The CINCINNATI BENGALS
and the Magic of Paul Brown

The CINCINNATI BENGALS

and the Magic of Paul Brown

by Dick Forbes

A Stuart L. Daniels Book

PRENTICE-HALL, INC.
Englewood Cliffs, New Jersey

THE CINCINNATI BENGALS
and the Magic of Paul Brown

by Dick Forbes

Published by Prentice-Hall, Inc.
Englewood Cliffs, New Jersey

Printed in the United States of America • T
Prentice-Hall International, Inc., London
Prentice-Hall of Australia, Pty. Ltd., Sydney
Prentice-Hall of Canada, Ltd., Toronto
Prentice-Hall of India Private Ltd., New Delhi
Prentice-Hall of Japan, Inc., Tokyo

ISBN: 0-13-133900-1 (paperbound)

ISBN: 0-13-133918-4 (hardbound)

Library of Congress Catalog Card Number: 73-7228

Photography by:
Chance Brockway
Malcolm W. Emmons

a dynamite team

It was the night of August 3, 1968, before a group of more than 21,000 fans, and a newly formed group of players holding an NFL franchise—the Cincinnati Bengals—took the field against one of the strongest teams in professional football—the Kansas City Chiefs.

A solitary figure stood on the Bengal sidelines. He was Paul Brown, renowned in contemporary football lore, a man whose contributions to pro football in the past three decades have been legion.

Although the result of the game between the novice Bengals and the seasoned Chiefs was predictable, Paul Brown had not expected otherwise. The Chiefs won easily, 38–14, and the defeat was so complete that the Bengals not only were held without a first down in the first half, but also were unable to run a play from scrimmage in the first quarter.

About a year after that fateful and hapless debut, the "Baby Bengals," as they were condescendingly called, faced the powerful Chiefs again. This time, however, with exhibition play behind them, the practice party was over and the Bengals were playing for keeps.

By 4:20 that afternoon, the infant team's initiation to the ranks of the pros was complete. Cincinnati had won, 24–19, and Paul Brown was carried off the field by his joyful charges as the crowd cheered wildly.

In just a little more than thirteen months the Bengals had beaten one of the best. That was the year Kansas City won the world championship and pro football came of age as a valuable commodity in Cincinnati, a city previously dominated by the Reds of baseball fame.

An Early Triumph

In the following seasons, Brown's "Baby Bengals" neatly divested themselves of that patronizing nickname. In 1970, their third year, with Virg Carter filling in for injured quarterback Greg Cook, the Bengals logged an incredible 8–6 record and ended the season as champions of the AFC's newly created Central Division.

Dave Lewis is one of the finest punters in the game, but he prefers to play quarterback.

8

In 1972 Ken Anderson was fifth in the AFC in passing.

Virgil Carter eyes a receiver downfield as he is given time to throw by an alert offensive lineman.

No other expansion team had ever improved so steadily as to win a division crown in just three years. The bitterness of their 17–0 loss to the Baltimore Colts in the AFC playoff game was tempered by the knowledge that they had been beaten by the best—Baltimore went on to win the world championship.

Up until the end of the 1972 season, the Bengals had secured twenty-seven victories, suffered forty-three defeats and tolerated one tie. To date no other NFL expansion team has equaled that record, nor has any other racked up two winning seasons in its first five years of existence. Cincinnati finished 8–6 in both 1970 and 1972.

Crowd Pleasers

Just as impressive as the team's ferocity and competitiveness on the field has been Cincinnati's attendance record. 60,284 fans, the largest crowd ever to see any sports event in metropolitan Cincinnati, watched the Bengals lose a 27–24 heartbreaker to the Cleveland Browns in October 1971. That same season 414,769 fans were on hand for seven home games, and the attendance in 1972 was higher by more than 10,000.

It is almost impossible to buy season tickets at the Bengals' Riverfront Stadium. The fans of other teams have been known to complain that three preseason games are also included in the price of a season ticket. No such gripe is heard in Cincinnati, where attendance and excitement at the three exhibition games easily match those of the regular season.

One of the biggest plusses for the Cincinnati franchise came during the realignment of the team in the 1970 merger between the American and National Football leagues. Cleveland, which was destined from the start to be an arch intrastate rival, moved into the Central Division with the Bengals. Their games have been memorable from the start.

In 1972, the two clubs decided to play a preseason game every year in addition to their two regular-season clashes, and to meet at a mid-state location. The automatic choice was Ohio State Stadium in Columbus.

A huge throng of more than 85,000 saw that initial struggle. The figure was matched by the crowd for the 1973 game—it was scheduled for August and was sold out by April.

The Trademark Is Youth

If the Bengals, under Paul Brown's masterful hand, have been noted in the last five years for anything besides speed, toughness and refusal to quit, it is for their youth. This has become a team trademark.

"From the beginning," Brown points out, "we went the route of youth by building the team with draft choices from the college world. In the long run, to a certain degree, it has helped us. We were determined to be patient and grow along with green personnel who, we believed, had the potential for future greatness. It has paid off."

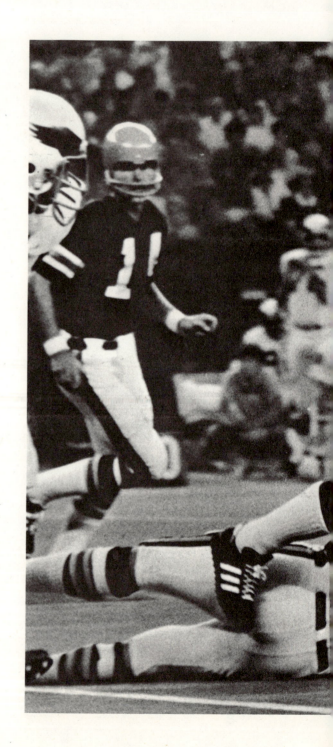

The "Essex Express" is also adept at catching passes. Here, he latches on to an eighteen-yarder thrown by Cincinnati quarterback Virg Carter.

Paul Brown is the greatest tactician the game has ever known.

paul brown -- master builder

Long-standing reports that Paul E. Brown went into virtual hibernation after his seventeen-year stand at Cleveland aren't exactly accurate. Bitter at the decision of the Browns' majority stockholder, Art Modell, to banish him from the team he founded in 1946 and led to great success, Brown moved bag and baggage to the beautiful seaside resort of La Jolla, California, and tried to settle down with his wife, Katie.

He was hardly desperate. His $80,000-per-year contract with the Browns had several seasons to run, and he had stock in the club, as well as profitable investments and land holdings. Paul and Katie traveled, once around the world. They moved into the nicely paced swing of La Jolla society. The coach played golf by day and bridge by night.

Paul Brown, founder, coach and general manager of the Bengals since their inception, watches the action on the field with a member of his team.

Larcenous Lemar Parrish steals Mike Phipps' pass as Ken Riley prepares to block.

A Firm Hold

But he kept alive in the pro football picture—or maybe it was that pro football made sure he kept up with it. He had several offers to coach other clubs. "Some of them came from the finest people in football," Brown says, "but none offered me exactly what I wanted—absolute control.

"I still believe the only really successful way to operate a franchise is to have just one top authority, and after what happened before [at Cleveland] I am more sure of it than ever. When a player or anyone else in the organization can go higher than the coach or general manager, it can only be chaos."

At Cincinnati, as both coach and general manager, Brown now has absolute authority, although his investment in the club, which is considerable, is still small compared to that of other stockholders. Brown's control comes from a voting trust, on which he insisted from the start, and which other stockholders—many of them Paul's personal friends—wanted as much as he did.

Two of Brown's three sons, Mike and Pete, are very much in the Bengals' organization and are keen football people. Mike, a former outstanding quarterback at Dartmouth, has a law degree from Harvard. He serves as assistant general manager and legal counsel and actually handles most of the inside duties for Paul, including player contracts. Pete is director of player personnel and his ability is shown in the results of the Bengals' drafts through the years. He also played football as a guard at Denison.

It was Mike Brown, during the period of his father's exile, who managed to keep check on future football possibilities while working for a Cleveland law firm during the mid-sixties. Both men knew that the NFL and the young American Football League eventually had to merge or spend themselves out of business, and that both leagues were interested in expanding beyond their most recent new cities, Atlanta and Miami.

Tommy Casanova receives congratulations from teammates and coach Paul Brown after a brilliant defensive play.

Guard Pat Matson checks the scoreboard from the bench.

Young Mike had been continually exploring possibilities and passing information along to Paul.

"One day Mike showed me a survey," Paul recalled, "that showed me that Cincinnati came on strong in many ways. The city not only was a huge metropolitan center of its own, but it was near other major centers—Dayton, Columbus, Louisville, Indianapolis and Lexington—all easily accessible by expressway.

"Besides that, Cincinnati's per capita income was higher than that of any other city we had previously checked, which was very much a major point."

With this information, Brown conferred with a wealthy Columbus veterinarian, Dr. Bill Hackett, who had formerly played for Brown at Ohio State.

"We sat around the pool and talked it all out," Brown said, "and finally determined that Bill would go back to Columbus and approach Jim Rhodes with the idea."

Rhodes was then governor of Ohio, keenly interested in upgrading the Buckeye State and bringing in new people and new business, and the idea appealed to him. Shortly thereafter, Brown was paid a visit by the governor—Cincinnati didn't know it at the time, but its pro football roots had been planted.

The New Franchise

Brown found backers for the club from the start. The problem was a stadium. When Paul and other club backers first approached the city fathers in Cincinnati about the franchise, there was no way such a proposal could be kept secret. It leaked out, and the possibilities of both a pro football franchise and a new stadium were front-page news from then on.

Even as early as 1964, Cincinnati's need for a new stadium, if for no other reason than to keep the baseball Reds in town, had been apparent. In May of that year an *Enquirer* columnist accused the city council of lack of leadership for standing flatfooted when there was imminent danger of losing the Reds to another city.

The bossman gives the signal—"One more play."

Paul Brown and his Green Bay counterpart, Dan Devine, share a joke before a game.

The old and the new—Cincinnati coach Paul Brown (right) and Miami coach Don Shula exchange a few pre-game remarks. Both men are considered to be geniuses in their field.

In September 1965, the same columnist rapped the city again for "doing nothing," this time for an added reason. Pro football's interest in the city had begun to leak out. There were straws in the wind.

The first step for the Bengals had begun in December 1965, before Paul Brown had even come into the picture. The city of Cincinnati announced that a new stadium would be built.

By March 1966, however, the secret was out. Brown told a Cincinnati writer that the city had "as much and probably more going for it than any of the other cities" seeking a franchise.

Cincinnati began working feverishly for an NFL franchise by the spring of 1966, not even considering the struggling American Football League, but once the two leagues announced merger plans, the question became academic. Sooner or later it would be all one league. When, on November 1, 1966, the NFL awarded its sixteenth franchise to New Orleans, Cincinnati's efforts were immediately directed toward getting a team in the AFL. By that time, both leagues had agreed on a complete merger by 1970.

No sooner had New Orleans been taken in by the NFL than Brown announced he was perfectly willing to accept an AFL franchise. In truth, he already had it.

The Tenth Team

However, even when the AFL named the Bengals its tenth team in late May 1967, with operations to begin in the 1968 season, there was still speculation as to who would operate the franchise. All the time, Brown, jetting back and forth between California and Cincinnati, was assured of getting the club. "I had it in my hip pocket," he said, "but we had to wait for the announcement."

Delay in picking a site for the stadium, not to mention the start of construction, continued to hold everything up. The city continued, in some ways, to twiddle its thumbs.

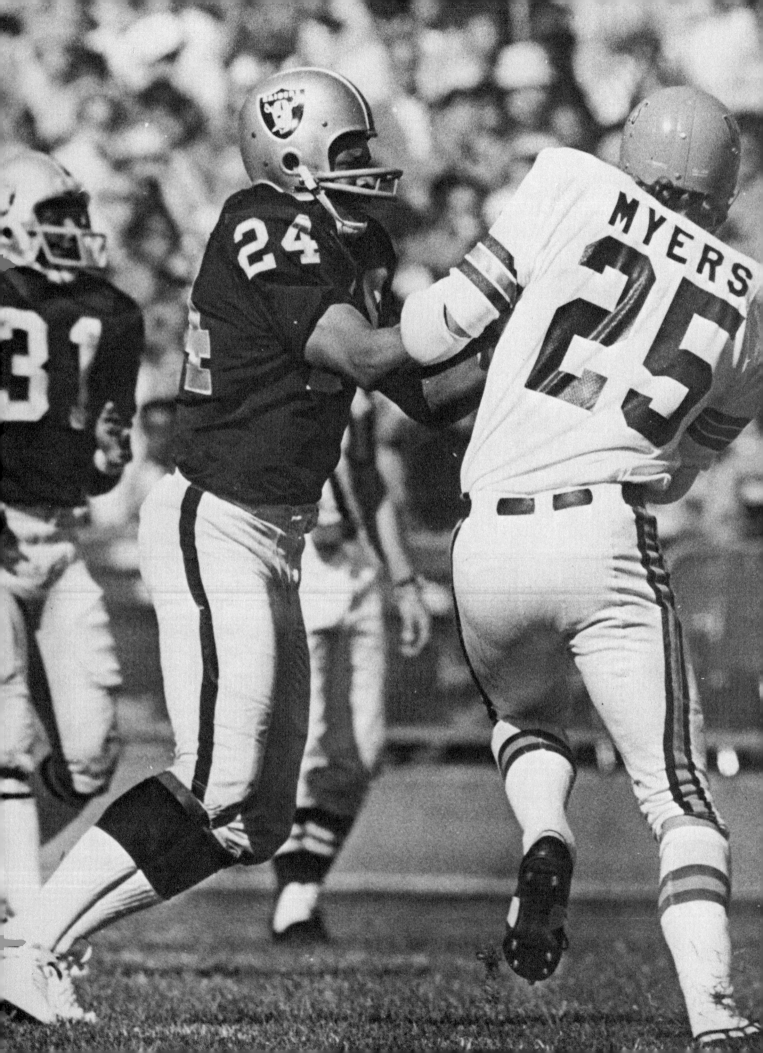

Tommy Casanova

Nonetheless, it was generally conceded that pro football had saved major-league baseball for Cincinnati. The city would never have undertaken to build a stadium for the Reds alone; it had to be assured of a pro football franchise. And the Reds, most assuredly, would have left had not the city promised them a new stadium. The two sports went hand in hand.

Ironically, in December 1966, when Reds' owner Bill DeWitt sold the club to a Cincinnati group that promised to keep the franchise in town, the buyers were almost the same people who were backing Paul Brown in football.

The AFL finally announced publicly, in July 1967, that the Cincinnati franchise had been awarded to Paul Brown. He accepted the job, even though he knew he would get the slimmest pickings ever offered a new team in pro football.

As he remembers it now, "We never received from the league as generous a start in the allocation of players as did Miami, New Orleans or Atlanta." And even at that he doesn't go far enough.

Whereas Miami received a guarantee of $500,000 in television money in its first year, the Cincinnati franchise received nothing in its first two seasons. Furthermore, transmission of NFL games into Cincinnati, chiefly those of the popular Cleveland Browns, continued, even when the Bengals were playing at home.

The Master's Return

As it turned out, the AFL's "announcement" that Brown had the franchise wasn't official in July of 1967. It wasn't until late September, after long meetings with AFL people over a myriad of details, that Paul finally signed. The meeting with Dr. Hackett had finally culminated in "the master's" return to pro football in Cincinnati.

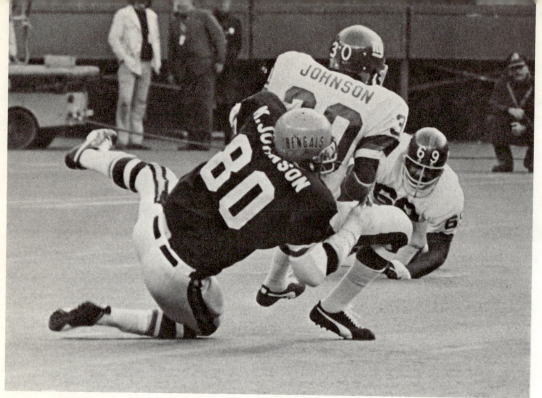

*Ken Johnson nabs Giant running back
Ron Johnson.*

*Bernard Jackson makes a valiant effort to
block Pete Gogolak's kick.*

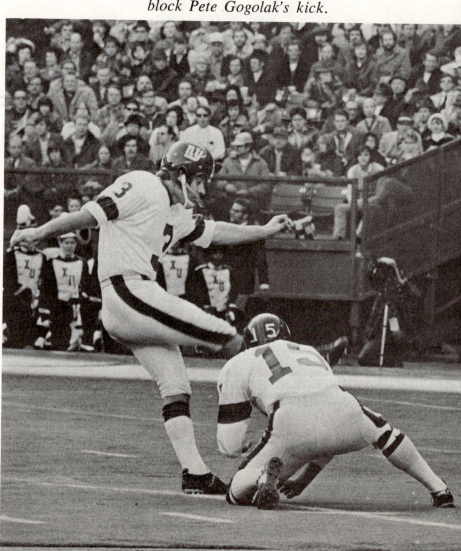

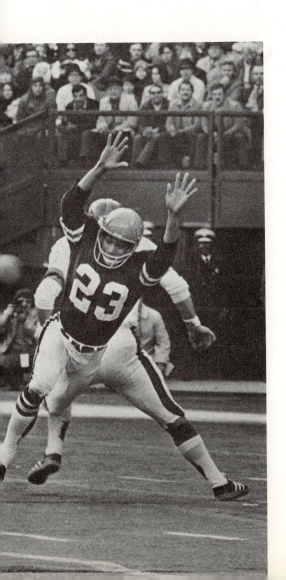

"I feel as if I'm breathing again," Brown said. "This is like coming home again. What an opportunity it is to build another one." But he warned his colleagues in the venture, "This is going to cost you a considerable sum of money." At the same time he warned both the AFL and NFL, "I'm not in this to get wiped out." As things have developed, there was no danger.

Brown went to work immediately. He began to assemble his coaching staff, including Al LoCasale as director of personnel, and LoCasale stayed two years before moving to Oakland, after which Pete Brown took the job.

Brown gave the name "Bengals" to the team, naming it after a previous Cincinnati NFL franchise that had lasted for three poorly attended years in the 1930s. The name also gave Paul the opportunity to use the initials "CB" on the coaching caps—"CB" also stood for Cleveland Browns.

Colors—and a Staff

The team's new colors, Brown said, would be orange, black and white. At Cleveland they were—and still are —orange, brown and white.

Allan Heim, then executive sports editor of *The Cincinnati Enquirer,* was appointed Director of Public Relations, and later in the month the club signed a forty-year lease to use the new stadium. Both the Bengals and the Reds, in 1970, moved to new offices at Riverfront, which was officially opened for baseball in June of that year.

Brown's first assistant coach, appointed defensive coordinator, was Tom Bass, who formerly had worked for Sid Gillman at San Diego. Rick Forzano from the St. Louis Cardinals was named to handle the offensive backs.

Three more were appointed soon after—Bill Johnson from San Francisco as offensive line coach, Jack (J. D.) Donaldson from the New York Jets as defensive line coach and Bill Walsh, who had formerly been with the Oakland Raiders, as receiver-quarterback coach. J. D.

Guard Steve Lawson (68) was a top draft pick in 1971 and has developed rapidly under coach Paul Brown.

Johnson and Walsh are still with Brown. Forzano re-signed after one year to become head coach at Navy, and Bass a year later because of poor health, though he still functions as the club's West Coast scout.

Brown increased his staff from five to six in 1969, naming his former All-Pro star at Cleveland, Vince Costello, to coach the linebackers. Donaldson moved over to the offensive backfield after Forzano's departure, and Chuck Studley, formerly head coach at the University of Cincinnati, took over the defensive line. When Bass left, Brown signed as his defensive coordinator Chuck Weber, another of his players from Cleveland, who had followed Bass as defensive chief with the Chargers before joining Cincinnati.

All six present assistants have worked with Brown since 1970, all obviously with one thing in mind: a crack at the Super Bowl.

Bengals' First Draft

At Jacksonville, Florida, in January 1968, the AFL held its allocation draft for the new Cincinnati franchise. The owners made sure, UPI reported, "that Brown doesn't start another dynasty [as he had at Cleveland] too soon."

Under the draft terms, each AFL team was allowed to freeze twenty-nine of its first forty players. After one pick from each team (Miami was excluded), the clubs could freeze two more. Two more Cincinnati picks, and the clubs again froze two more players.

After one more freeze, and one more player selection, each team would then "award" the Bengals one more player. As one AFL owner reported later, "It's like the inscription on the Statue of Liberty: 'Give me your tired, your poor, your homeless. . . .'" He couldn't have been more right.

Wide receiver Speedy Thomas holds the Bengals' single-game receiving mark, with seven catches for 177 yards against Denver in 1969.

Jess Phillips has been a dependable and consistent running back for the Bengals.

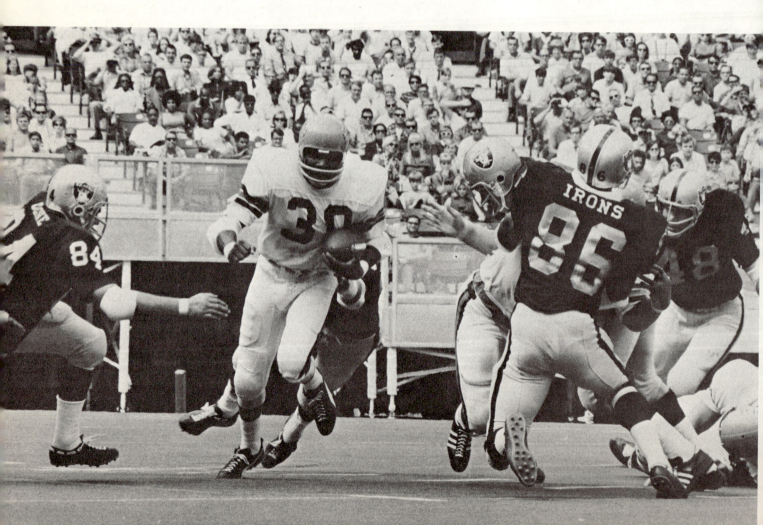

One of the Bengals coaches gets his point across to defensive lineman Bill Bergey.

Of the original forty, only eight were still around by the time the Bengals opened their regular season in 1968, and today there is just one, guard Pat Matson, who also is the players' representative for the NFL Players' Association. Matson, a standout at Oregon, came to the club from Denver.

The first twenty-six-team college draft in the joint NFL-AFL draft was held on January 31 and February 1, 1968, with the Cincinnati franchise given some special help. After one first-round choice, in which All-American center Bob Johnson from Tennessee became the first player ever taken by Cincinnati, the club received two selections in the second round, three in the third, two in the fourth, one in the fifth, etc.

Five years later, of the forty-one collegians chosen by the Bengals, just six remained—Bob Johnson, running back Jess Phillips, linebacker Al Beauchamp, tackle Howard Fest, running back Essex Johnson and tight end Bob Trumpy. A half dozen others made the team but were eventually traded.

Only a week after the draft, Brown spoke at a "get-acquainted" luncheon in Cincinnati, and the tone was optimistic.

"If you stick with us, feel good when we win and down when we lose, I think we can have a good time of it. Don't feel sorry for me. I went into this because I wanted to. It's my life. Everything so far has gone according to plan."

Speedy Jess Phillips scampers through an opening in the Oakland line.

Welcome to Pro Football

Two weeks later, at the first combined AFL-NFL owners' meeting in New York, Cincinnati was given an official welcome into pro football. And one AFL representative finally revealed their inner feelings about Paul Brown's new venture: "The AFL needed Cincinnati badly . . . a city in the heart of the population center of the United States. It was one of the things the league lacked."

"Rams Face No-Names on Sunday," declared a headline in a Los Angeles newspaper in October 1972. To a certain extent it was true, and hardly unexpected of an expansion team. Nevertheless, the Bengals have contributed some stars to pro football already, and there are other players on the brink of national fame. In Cincinnati some of them are household words already.

Paul Brown's ambitious "five-year plan," begun in 1968, had quickly outgrown itself. "We plan to be completely competitive in five years," he had told a preseason crowd in the late summer of 1968. His prediction proved overly conservative, as the Bengals opened their second year with consecutive victories over Miami and San Diego and capped the season with their astounding upset of Kansas City.

"That was the first time our people began to realize we could beat anybody," Brown remembers proudly. "I guess you could say that was 'the end of the beginning.'"

As Ken Anderson fades back to pass, line-men Howard Fest (72) and Bob Johnson (54) stay in position to block for him.

promise and disappointment

In 1968, a quarterback named Greg Cook was running the University of Cincinnati attack, playing on the same Nippert Stadium turf that the Bengals used on Sundays. Cook, an Ohio product from nearby Chillicothe, led the nation's major college division in total offense and passing.

Cook was a phenomenon in every respect. A great athlete with a rifle-like arm to match, he was a natural quarterback with a fierce, competitive flair with which to inspire his teammates. On several Saturday afternoons in 1968, Paul Brown sat in Nippert Stadium with members of his coaching staff and watched Greg perform miracles behind an offensive line that was only nominally efficient.

In his old coaching days with the Cleveland Browns, cagey Paul always liked to have hometown products around—or players from Ohio, if he could get them. He picked up Don Shula from John Carroll and Warren Lahr from Western Reserve, just to name a couple from Cleveland campuses.

Now he saw a chance to repeat a successful pattern by picking a prized quarterback right in the Bengals' own backyard. Could he get Cook? He knew it would be tough, particularly since the Bengals finished their first year with a 3–11 record. Bad as it was, even for a first-year team, the Bengals' tally was not rock bottom— four other NFL clubs, including two of the oldest and most solid teams, had finished beneath them.

The Bengals had fifth pick after Buffalo, Atlanta, Philadelphia and Pittsburgh. Would Cook last that long? Brown gambled that he would, and the Cincinnati draft in 1969 was predicated on getting him. Luckily there were four other highly regarded college prospects, although none of them was a quarterback, always the highest prize.

Brown's intuition was that the other clubs' needs would be primarily in other positions, and his hunch was right.

After O. J. Simpson, George Kunz and Leroy Keyes had been picked off by Buffalo, Atlanta and Philadelphia, respectively, the Steelers selected giant-sized defensive tackle Joe Greene, and Cincinnati's choice was clear. From the moment the Bengals chose Greg Cook, the team's future in the NFL was thought to be assured.

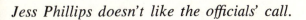
Jess Phillips doesn't like the officials' call.

*Second-round draft choice Bill Bergey was
a Little-All-American at Arkansas State.*

Ken Riley is a member of the highly touted Cincinnati secondary.

The Exhibition Games

Cook's first start for the Bengals, in exhibition play against Kansas City, was anything but auspicious as the Chiefs won 23–7. But the next week it was different.

In the last football game ever played in old Forbes Field in Pittsburgh, Cook completed eight of eleven passes for 158 yards and one touchdown, and his passing set up scores in four of the first five times the Bengals had the ball in a 23–13 victory over the Steelers.

In four exhibition games, Cook had completed fifty of seventy-nine passes for a phenomenal 63.3 percent, better than any of the quarterbacks the Bengals were to face during the regular 1969 season—Len Dawson, Bob Griese, Daryle Lamonica, Joe Namath, John Hadl, Pete Beathard, Steve Tensi, Mike Taliaferro, and Jack Kemp.

The Season Opens

The 1969 Bengals finished a nominal 3–2 exhibition season to open at home against Miami. They were feeling good, and it wasn't all because of Greg Cook. Three rookies had helped add a lot of quickness and muscle to the defense: middle linebacker Bill Bergey from Arkansas State, defensive end Royce Berry from Houston and cornerback Ken Riley from Florida A&M.

Additionally, wide receiver Speedy Thomas out of Utah and guard Guy Dennis from Florida had helped the offense, and soccer-style kicker Horst Muhlmann from Germany, acquired from the Chiefs in a trade for Warren McVea, added a recognized scoring threat.

The home opener against the Dolphins was notable for more reasons than a 27–21 Bengal victory, in which Cook threw two touchdown passes to Eric Crabtree; it was the 300th win for coach Paul Brown and an impressive Cincinnati debut for kicker Muhlmann.

Royce Berry has been a mainstay of the defensive line since he joined the club in 1969.

Both Lemar Parrish and his backfield mate, Tommy Casanova, returned punts for touchdowns in 1972.

The Cincinnati fans are predominantly German in origin, just as they are Swedish in Minneapolis and Irish in Boston, and they cheered everything Muhlmann did— his two field goals, his three extra points and his kick-offs out of the end zone, one of which hit the very top of a goal post. The redhead from Gelsenkerchen, West Germany, was a hit from the start.

The second game of the season produced a 34–20 victory over the strong San Diego Chargers and was one of the biggest in Cincinnati history. Cook pitched three touchdowns to as many receivers, ran eight yards himself for another one and completed fourteen of twenty-two passes for 327 yards. Muhlmann, adding insult to injury, kicked two field goals. It was one of San Diego coach Sid Gillman's most humiliating defeats.

Unfortunately, the Bengals' victory was clouded by injury. The team was still a year away from its new Riverfront Stadium home, and, in the tiny confines of Nippert Stadium, tight end Bruce Coslet caught a touch-down pass, ran into a concrete wall and suffered a cracked kneecap.

A Serious Setback

The third game, against the Kansas City Chiefs, was won 24–19, but it was a shocker of the first caliber for a variety of reasons other than the fact that it was the Bengals' third straight victory.

What happened that fateful afternoon has been felt by the Bengals ever since and has been called by Paul Brown "one of the club's two biggest setbacks in its five-year history."

Early in the second quarter, those massive Chief defenders Willie Lanier and Bobby Bell sacked Cook for a seven-yard loss, and Greg didn't get up. When the medics finally got him on his feet and helped him to the sidelines, a tragic episode began for the Bengals.

Running back Jess Phillips was the Bengals' leading ground gainer in 1969 and 1970.

An integral part of the Bengal defense— end Sherman White.

The loss of Cook brought forth quarterback Sam Wyche, who came to the Bengals as a walk-on free agent from Furman. Despite a broken ankle suffered in Miami in 1969, Wyche connected on an eighty-yard touchdown pass to Eric Crabtree, and set Jess Phillips up for a ten-yard winning touchdown on an up-the-middle play.

At that point in the season Cincinnati stood at 3–0 but had yet to play away from home. Their next game was a rematch with the Chargers at San Diego, and Paul Brown knew that Sid Gillman would have his players "high as a Georgia pine" for the little expansion team that had so rudely trounced them just a couple of weeks earlier.

Sam Wyche was the starting quarterback. Just to be on the safe side, Brown activated John Stofa, a quarterback he had first signed in January 1968 and a refugee from the Dolphins.

The Bengals blitzed the Chargers with a four-play touchdown drive to start the game, but San Diego wasn't taking the Bengals lightly this time. They held a 14–7 lead going into the third quarter, and although Cincinnati fought back to a 14–14 tie, the honeymoon was over for the Bengals when John Hadl drove his team seventy-seven yards down the field for a final-quarter touchdown.

They were to lose, successively, to the world-champion Jets, the Denver Broncos and, once again, to Kansas City, who crushed them 42–22. Cincinnati then stood at 3–4, exactly where an expansion team in its second year is expected to stand.

During this string of losses, Cook had tried to play against the Jets, but he found out quickly that he wasn't up to it. The handwriting was on the wall, though the picture would not be finally clear until the following season.

A Challenge Is Met

As November opened, the undefeated Raiders loomed as the Bengals' most serious challenge to date. Prospects were not bright for the team that had failed to win a game in October. But there was one ray of hope—Greg Cook seemed ready to play again.

The Bengals surged to a 24–0 halftime lead and handed the Raiders a crushing 31–17 defeat, their only loss in the entire season. Among those who shared in the heroics, Cook contributed eleven of nineteen pass completions for 189 yards and two touchdown passes to young Chip Myers. It was the offensive line's best day.

From the defensive standpoint, the game had its other aspects. For one thing, Raider quarterback Daryle Lamonica threw five interceptions, a result of continual biting pressure from the defensive line and sharp work in the backfield. Cornerback Fletcher Smith himself intercepted two passes.

And there was something else—another harbinger of impending doom—Cook's arm tightened up badly in the second half, and he threw only seven times, with three completions.

Deadlock at Houston

Next came a date with the Oilers in the Astrodome, a monumental offensive show that ended in a 31–31 tie, the only deadlock the Bengals have played in their five years.

The statistics favored Houston all the way. The Oilers piled up 456 yards with twenty-six first downs and gained 237 yards on the ground alone. But there was an equalizer Houston was powerless to overcome—Greg Cook, who, in his greatest performance as a pro, connected on fifteen of twenty-five passes for 298 yards and threw four touchdown passes, three to Bob Trumpy and another to Eric Crabtree.

*Courage has been Virgil Carter's trade-
mark.*

The Bengals have the tallest pass-catching corps in football. Tight end Bruce Coslet (88) is six-foot-three.

Howard Fest, who has been switched back and forth from guard to tackle, is one of the original Bengals.

After that performance, neither Cook nor the rest of the team was able to reach the form they had shown in those back-to-back games with Oakland and Houston, and the rest of the 1969 season was all downhill. They suffered successive losses to Boston, the Jets, Buffalo, Oakland and Denver.

However, the 4–9–1 record was a slight improvement on the Bengals' first season, and Cincinnati expected a sensational year as they moved into Riverfront Stadium for the 1970 campaign. For obvious reasons, their plans were built around Cook.

Although he had finished out the 1969 season, it soon became apparent during the summer that Cook wasn't going to be available for 1970. Nor has he been available since then. In 1973 he tried again, but after two weeks in summer camp the pain proved too much to bear. Now, after three shoulder operations and a three-year absence from football, it appears that Cook's playing days are definitely over.

*The Bengal offensive line is about to en-
counter the Miami defensive line.*

49

Arizonan Paul Robinson demonstrates his superior running talents against the hapless New Orleans Saints. Robinson played for the Bengals 'til the middle of the 1972 season when he was traded to Houston.

division champions

There were two major problems that loomed for 1970. Paul Robinson, rookie-of-the-year in 1968, failed to play up to expectations in 1969, although one reason was the emphasis on the passing attack. Robinson, a running back from Arizona, who had played football only in his senior year, ran for more than 1,000 yards in 1968. He never came close again, and the "Cactus Comet" had one weakness in common with other offensive backs—he couldn't catch the ball. Invariably it was thrown to receivers or the tight end, as the defensive backs knew well. In 1972 Robinson was traded to Houston, along with another running back, Fred Willis.

The other major problem was defense. The Bengals gave up almost 400 yards per game (381.3), and there was no question as to where the major emphasis would be in the 1970 draft. They needed defensive help.

And so, in 1970, into Bengalland came the piano-playing Pennsylvanian Mike Reid, a 255-pound defensive tackle from Penn State. He was a first-round choice, and defensive tackle Ron Carpenter from North Carolina State was taken in the second round. Today these two form much of the nucleus of a stern Bengal defense that was second only to the Miami Dolphins in the 1972 American Conference season.

Reid, All-Pro for the preceding two years, made everyone's All-America team. He won the Outland Trophy in 1969 as the outstanding college lineman. Quick as a cat, and with feline footwork to match, Reid was part and parcel of a Bengal team that surprised the pro football world in 1970.

But by far the most overlooked and underrated player in Bengal history was a six-foot, baby-faced quarterback named Virg Carter, a former All-American and leading college passer at Utah.

Despite the heroics of Sam Wyche, who again was destined for more hero laurels in 1970, the "Furman flinger" was not a starter. Jim Del Gaizo, a tough little scrambler signed on as a free agent from Tampa, and big Dave Lewis, a combination quarterback-punter from Stanford, didn't measure up as first-liners, either. Del Gaizo was waived before the season started, and Lewis, also a free agent who had spent some time with the New York Giants and in the Canadian League, stayed on as a punter—a role in which he led the NFL in both 1970 and 1971—and as backup quarterback.

Carter for Quarterback

One day in mid-August, two quarterbacks appeared in camp simultaneously—Virg Carter and a handsome Southerner named Bob Davis, who had great college credentials at Virginia as well as some pro experience with Houston and the New York Giants.

Running back Doug Dressler resolutely holds on to the football as an enemy hand reaches in to grab it. Center Bob Johnson blocks.

Bill Bergey confers with Cincinnati defensive lineman Mike Reid.

52

Chip Myers isn't posing, but he certainly makes this catch look picture-perfect.

After two days of testing and watching, Brown and his staff made a decision. They kept Carter and cut Davis. It was one of the best moves Brown ever made, although for the first half of the regular 1970 season many doubted his wisdom. Among them, naturally, were sportswriters.

Carter, who led the nation in total offense at Utah in 1966, was drafted by the Chicago Bears in '67. On the taxi squad for his first pro season, Virg made the Bears' varsity the following year and in 1969 actually started five games, all of which ended in Chicago victories.

But Carter couldn't get along with either George Halas or the Bears' coaching staff, at one point accusing them of not keeping promises, and, during the winter of 1969–70, he was shuffled off to Buffalo. It seemed to be the end of the line for Carter when the Bills put him on waivers that summer. Little did he know what joining Paul Brown and the Bengals would mean before the season was over.

Cincinnati's pre-season campaign in 1970 was inauspicious—a mere 2–3–1. The Bengals had walloped the Cleveland Browns 31–24 in the initial meeting between the new archrivals. But the last two games had resulted in a 10–10 tie with a so-so Green Bay squad that had not yet started to rebuild under coach Dan Devine, and a 31–14 defeat at the hands of the Detroit Lions.

1970 Opening

With Sam Wyche still starting at quarterback and Carter still learning the intricacies of the offense, the Bengals opened the 1970 season with yet another surprise. With a 31–21 triumph, they smashed Oakland, the team that had posted a 12–1–1 regular-season mark in 1969, whipped Houston 56–7 in the playoffs and lost only to Kansas City for the last American Football League championship.

Middle linebacker Bill Bergey, here giving himself a refreshing bath, has been the Bengals' leading tackler from 1970 to 1972.

Doug Dressler drives up the middle against Cleveland, breaking the tackle of linebacker Billy Andrews.

It was an auspicious start that made Wyche appear to be deeply entrenched as starting quarterback, and the rookies at tackle on the defensive line—Mike Reid and Ron Carpenter—looked like guards at Fort Knox.

But the victory did not go unnoticed in Detroit, where the Bengals had to play on the following Sunday, and coach Joe Schmidt had his Lions ready. They whipped Cincinnati 38–3 in a one-sided game remembered, at least in Detroit, for one thing.

The Lions had not been scored upon in the previous week, and with only one play to go against Cincinnati they were within reach of posting eight shutout quarters —one of professional football's rarest feats.

But Brown put a slight blemish on the victory when he ordered Horst Muhlmann to try a twenty-seven-yard field goal, which he successfully kicked just before the finish. Paul Brown was roundly booed by Detroit fans as he walked off the field.

Later, asked why he had called for a field goal, Brown wryly answered, "It's the object of the game to put points on the board, isn't it?"

The loss to Detroit began a string of six straight defeats, including a 30–27 heartbreaker to the Browns at Cleveland in the first regular-season meeting between the teams in the new NFL realignment. It marked the first appearance of Paul Brown in Cleveland since the Browns' owner, Art Modell, had fired him at the end of the 1962 season.

Brown was greeted by hundreds of friends at Cleveland, and, as he admitted both before and afterwards, "It will be—and was—an emotional experience." But the Browns, who bore his name, did not allow emotion to distract them from the task at hand.

The six-game losing streak also included defeats by Houston, Kansas City, Washington and Pittsburgh. The 20–0 loss to the Redskins was one of only three games in Cincinnati history in which the team went without scoring.

The Cleveland game, the fourth of the season, marked an abrupt change in the Bengal offense, although the effects weren't to show until later. It was Virg Carter's debut as a starting quarterback. Brown was convinced that a change had to be made, and the twenty-seven points that Carter helped produce bore him out.

Misery at Midpoint

Nevertheless, at the halfway point of the 1970 season, the Bengals had won exactly one game. They had lost six straight. They were losing, invariably, with defensive breakdowns. In seven straight games they had yielded anywhere from twenty to thirty-eight points.

At that point in the season anyone who had even suggested that the Bengals would go on to win the AFC-Central would summarily have been declared a candidate for the psycho ward. And yet there were straws in the wind.

Other division teams were having an almost equally bad time. Houston appeared to be hopelessly out of the race, and Cleveland and Pittsburgh could never have been able to establish a clear-cut lead. Of course, the Bengals' cause seemed almost as hopeless too.

But in game number eight against Buffalo, the Bengal defense came alive. The Bills were held to fourteen points, Cincinnati's best defensive game of the year, and Carter came into his own by throwing three touchdown passes. Suddenly the Bengal offense began to show some tooth and claw. Their forty-three points against Buffalo were the most any Cincinnati team ever had scored to that point.

On the following Sunday, the Cleveland Browns made their first regular-season visit to Riverfront Stadium, and the Bengals were waiting. With a close-to-the-vest offense and a brutal, crushing defense, they put down the Browns, 14–10, the only victory they have ever scored over Cleveland in the regular campaign. It was a springboard that helped spur the Bengals to seven straight victories and their first division title.

Running back Ron Lamb, one of the top special teams' men in pro football, is an aggressive, hard tackler.

Without doubt Dave Lewis is one of the best punters in the NFL, having led the league in 1970 and 1971.

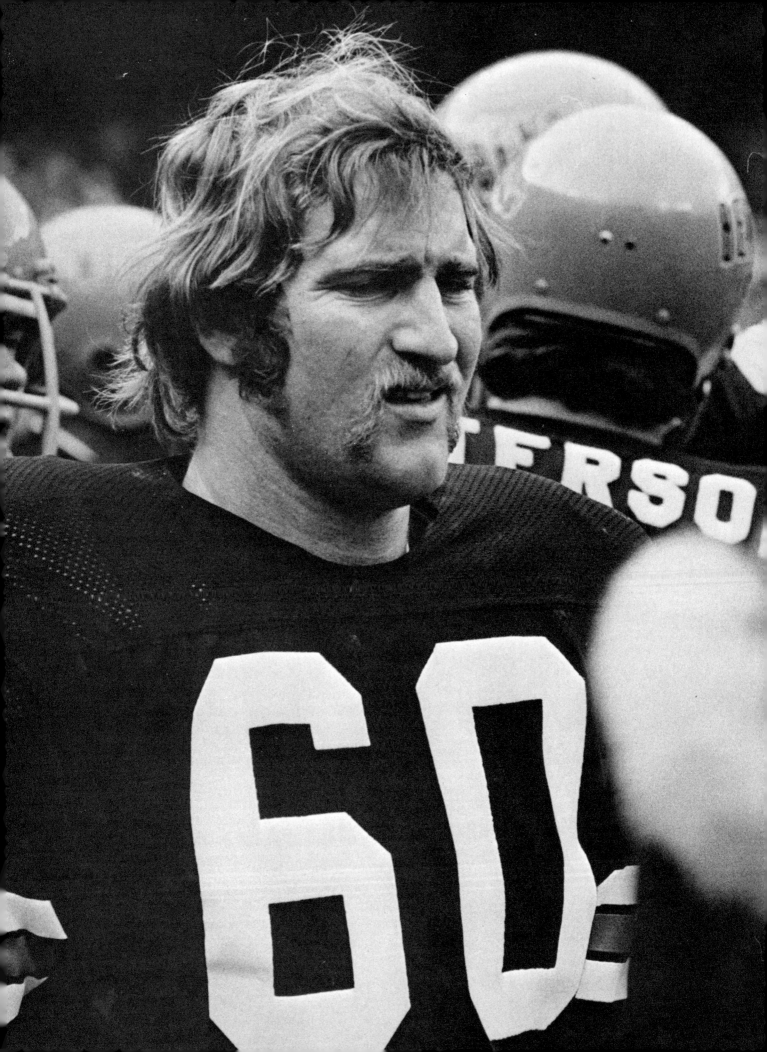

Linebacker Ron Pritchard was traded from Houston to Cincinnati in the middle of the 1972 season.

The Tables Are Turned

After the Cleveland game, the remaining schedule was almost made to order. Pittsburgh and New Orleans were at home, San Diego and Houston were away and Boston would end the season in Riverfront. Carter was coming into his own, and the defense was growing tougher game by game.

In retrospect, defense made the difference. The drafting of Mike Reid and Ron Carpenter was paying dividends, sophomores middle linebacker Bill Bergey and defensive end Royce Berry were playing splendidly, and others such as Al Beauchamp and New York Giants "transfer" Ken Avery were making Cincinnati linebackers tough to deal with.

Additionally, the defensive backfield was finally beginning to jell behind regulars Ken Dyer, Ken Riley and Fletcher Smith, along with rookies Sandy Durko from Southern California and a great natural athlete named Lemar Parrish from tiny Lincoln University.

The rebirth of the defense showed at the end of the regular season. Over the first seven games Cincinnati had given up 177 points, or 25.3 per game. But in the final seven they allowed just 78 points, or 11.1 per game.

The Bengals took Pittsburgh and New Orleans apart, then headed for the big game with San Diego on the coast. As usual, Sid Gillman had his Chargers on the heels of Oakland and Kansas City.

The 17–14 Cincinnati victory was one of the big ones in Bengal history. "I'd say that was a decided turning point in view of the way we won it," Paul Brown says now.

"The way we won it" is remembered by veteran Bengals to this day. Against a ferocious Charger pass rush, Virg Carter's passing produced not a single first down, and at game's end the Cincinnati record showed a loss of five yards. Nevertheless, the Bengals had won, and the credit—as always in a close game—went to the defense.

Gillman was astounded. Because of a stomach ailment, he had temporarily turned the field command over to an assistant coach, though Gillman still steered the play from a booth in the press box. At halftime, with the Chargers trailing 14–7, Gillman turned to a member of the Cincinnati contingent and declared:

"We're gonna stop fooling around now. We're gonna clean your plow."

But what the Bengal defense didn't do to blunt Gillman's threat, Horst Muhlmann and Dave Lewis did. Muhlmann kicked a twenty-eight-yard field goal to provide the winning margin, Cincinnati's only score in the second half, and Lewis continually kept the Chargers at bay with a series of dazzling, long punts. He averaged more than fifty-three yards for the day.

The following week, as the Bengals settled down to practice for their yearly engagement with Houston in the Astrodome, Carter was the hero of the day. The Bengals were very much in the thick of the race, but they had to keep on winning.

Brown made the most of Carter's inspirational leadership and physical assets. The offense was tailored to his talents: the down-and-out pass, the short hitches, the hooks, his dipsy-do faking on handoffs that made the running combination of Jess Phillips and Paul Robinson one to be feared. Phillips and Robinson ended almost even with more than 600 yards for the season, and so well did they blend that defenses did not dare key on one over the other.

Defensive end Royce Berry lunges at Miami running back Mercury Morris.

The Cincinnati defense intercepted twenty passes and returned them for 326 yards and three touchdowns in 1972.

Pat Matson is an integral part of Paul Brown's "pulling guard" offense because of his speed. Here he runs interference for Jess Phillips.

Additionally, Carter himself was an ever-present sprint-out threat, once breaking away on a seventy-two-yard run.

Besides all this, the quarterback had courage, and at Houston he was to prove it. Early in the second quarter, Carter caught his tongue between his teeth, was hit in the jaw by someone's helmet, and sprawled on the ground with his tongue almost split in half.

As Sam Wyche, always-ready Sam, rushed on the field, Carter was turned over to the team physicians, doctors George Ballou and Wally Timperman. First, the blood had to be stopped, and a wound in the mouth is the most difficult of all cuts to handle.

But they got the job done, and as the second half started, Carter was back in the huddle again, with seven stitches in a tongue so swollen that Paul Brown's messenger guards had to call the signals for him as they came running in from the bench. Carter was lucky to be able to count cadence.

But Virg played, the Bengals put down Houston 30–20 for their sixth straight victory, and all that remained for a Central Division title was a win over Boston. No matter what Cleveland did in its final game, the Browns were out of it if Cincinnati won. Pittsburgh had long since fallen from contention.

As Paul Brown recalls now, going into that game with the Patriots, with Riverfront sold out three weeks before, "We were literally afire. We lacked some things, but we had enthusiasm, and I honestly felt in my own mind we were over the hump. Yet, in pro football you never know, and we couldn't take Boston for granted."

Former All-American Ron Carpenter wraps up Cleveland quarterback Mike Phipps.

Paul Robinson, the first running back to gain 1,000 yards in his rookie year (1968), played his last game for Cincinnati in 1972.

Linebacker Ken Avery has the look of a man about to make contact with the opposition.

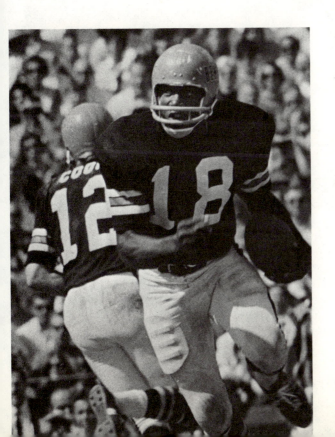

The Bengals most certainly didn't take the Patriots "for granted." With the division championship looking as big as the Super Bowl at that point ("the dollar-sign bowl," Bill Bergey called it), the Bengals swarmed over the Patriots 45–7 for the club's most one-sided victory to date.

In just three years, the Bengals had made the playoffs! The happy ending that would have completed the Cinderella story didn't come about, of course. On a cold day at Memorial Stadium in Baltimore, the Colts were just too good. Virg Carter, still bothered by his sore tongue and having been barely able to eat for two weeks, couldn't perform a second miracle on top of the first.

The Colts scored first, and played a very conservative game the rest of the way for a 17–0 victory, the last time the Bengals have been shut out to date.

Baltimore, with one of its greatest teams, went on to win the world championship, ripping Oakland 27–17 for the AFC title and finally taming the heavily favored Dallas Cowboys, 16–13, in the Super Bowl.

The success of the 1970 season was, in a way, one of the greatest ironies of all for the Cincinnati franchise. Looking back at five years of Bengal history, the man who made the club—Paul Brown—said recently, "The biggest setbacks we've had were losing Greg Cook and winning the divisional title in 1970.

"The loss of Cook, considering the potential he showed as a rookie, speaks for itself. But the divisional title kept us from the high draft-choice position in 1971 that we normally would have had."

Crafty wide receiver Chip Myers slips be-tween two Giant defenders, Otto Brown (21) and Pete Athas (45), and leaps high for the reception.

one step backward

The Bengals had the fifteenth pick in 1971, and any dreams of capturing blue-chippers for the "skilled positions" were shattered. Instead, they decided to go for offensive help up front.

Not only did they prove highly successful once more, but it is difficult to guess how their 1971 draft could have been any better under the circumstances. The first four draftees became starters, although not all in the first year. Five of the first six selections were good enough to make the club's regular roster, and the eleventh-round choice, wide receiver Ed Marshall, stayed with the cab squad and was activated late in the season.

Tackle Vernon Holland, a first-round draft choice in 1971, has the potential to become one of the best offensive linemen in the NFL.

The first-round selection was mountain-sized offensive tackle Vern Holland from Tennessee State, a talented and likable athlete who made the starting lineup almost immediately. Brown thinks Holland, just now coming into his own, "is a certain star of the future."

Guard Steve Lawson from Kansas, drafted in the second round, has been an in-again, out-again regular for two years, being plagued by injuries. Brown thinks Lawson "has every chance" of becoming a starter in 1973 if he can stay healthy during the training season.

The third-round choice was a real surprise, except, perhaps, to the real insiders of the game, the pro scouts.

The Bengals went for a six-foot-two, 205-pound quarterback named Ken Anderson, the first football player ever drafted from tiny Augustana College in Rockford, Illinois. Anderson had been carefully checked by any number of Bengal scouts, who found him up to every physical qualification. Their only question was whether he could rise to pro standards after playing a completely unsophisticated brand of college football—whether he could withstand the inevitable physical beating and mental stresses.

The early selection of Anderson was, indeed, even more of a gamble than was taking Greg Cook in the first round. Greg had played in a far superior league against far superior opponents.

Brown knew that Anderson was a draft for the future, but he didn't know, then, how soon the future was to be.

Running back Fred Willis from Boston College, taken in the fourth round, was used extensively in both 1971 and '72, sometimes as a starter, until he and longtime Bengal favorite Paul Robinson were traded to Houston midway in the '72 season.

Neil Craig, a cornerback from Fisk and a Cincinnati native, the seventh-round choice, also made the club and has improved tremendously in just two years.

Preseason Plays

Coming out of a seven-game winning streak, not counting the playoff loss to Baltimore, the Bengals were determined to keep going at full blast as they started the preseason schedule in 1971. They swept through the exhibitions: Miami (later to play in the Super Bowl), Detroit, Pittsburgh, St. Louis and, finally, Green Bay went down successively before the Bengals. The fur was flying.

Cincinnati played the last game of the exhibition season against the Washington Redskins, a team pulling itself together after a thorough housecleaning by new coach George Allen, a keen observer who sensed that the Bengals were tired. This string of twelve victories in the last thirteen starts had taken its toll. Nevertheless, they managed a 17–17 tie to finish the stern preseason campaign undefeated.

Virg Carter had become the number-one quarterback, Wyche had been traded to Washington during the off-season and young Ken Anderson was playing in the backup position, with Dave Lewis having been relegated to third place.

The Omens Were Good

When Cincinnati opened the season by trouncing the Eagles 37–14, the sky seemed almost the limit. It was the Bengals' thirteenth victory in fifteen consecutive games. Never had they looked more impressive.

Carter picked the Eagles' defense to shreds, hitting on twenty-two of thirty-three passes for 273 yards and three touchdowns, and Anderson—in the late stages—added two of three for thirty-seven yards more. Neither passer had been intercepted.

Backup safety Neil Craig is awaiting his chance.

Avery is on the move to get his man, Pittsburgh quarterback Terry Hanratty.

Essex Johnson, a twisting, cutting, high-speed running back who had been laboring in the shadows of Jess Phillips and Paul Robinson for three years, got his first start and made sure no one would forget it. He ran eight times for 113 yards, including a sixty-eight-yard touchdown romp on a pitchout from Carter.

Defensively, Mike Reid was a one-man gang. He sacked Eagle quarterback Pete Liske four times and the next day found himself nominated for rookie-of-the-year by a Philadelphia writer.

But happiness in the first game does not make a season, and this 1971 campaign was to become one of the most unfortunate of all for a Cincinnati team that had championship aspirations. It started the very next week in a 21–10 loss to the up-and-coming Pittsburgh Steelers, and even in that game problems showed up.

Late in August, in an exhibition game against the Cardinals, the Bengals had been hurt when wide receiver Chip Myers suffered two broken arms in a single crushing tackle. Fortunately, neither injury was excessive and Chip got back in action before mid-season. But he was not the Myers of the previous year, when he had been named All-Pro and had played in the Pro Bowl.

Then, in the third game of the season against Green Bay—a 20–17 loss—tragedy struck deep in the Bengals' camp.

Dyer Is Down

Very early in the game safety Ken Dyer, a tall, wiry athlete with the heart of a lion, tried to make a head-on tackle against mammoth Packer fullback John Brockington. They carried Dyer off the field to a hospital, and for weeks, at first fearing for his life, they felt he might never walk again. He was paralyzed from the shoulders down for several days with a snapped vertebra near his neck, and it was some time before he could move even his arms. Luckily, Ken could eat and talk, and his mind was unaffected.

Holland challenges Cleveland linebacker Jim Houston.

Quickness and agility give tackle Ron Carpenter extremely good range.

Bill Bergey intently watches the action from the sidelines.

The famous Paul Brown scowl.

Shortly before Christmas in 1971, after constant attention and expressions of friendship from the people of Green Bay, and after frequent visits from the Packers, including Brockington and coach Dan Devine, Dyer walked out of the hospital.

Within a year he had almost regained full mobility, although he will never play football again. During the 1972 exhibition season, Dyer returned to Green Bay for a Bengals game and, with his wife and new son, walked on the field at halftime to thunderous applause from 50,000 Green Bay fans.

It was the spirit of pro football at its best.

Dyer's loss, although by far the most serious, wasn't the only blow the Bengals received from the Packers. Virg Carter went down with a shoulder separation, and for the next several games rookie Ken Anderson, who only the year before had starred at Augustana College, became the quarterback of record. Several other injuries were suffered by the Bengals in that game, a pattern that was to continue for the rest of the season.

Despite the loss to Green Bay and the next week's 23–13 bow to Miami, the Bengals remained in contention. But if it wasn't injuries, it was foolish mistakes, and if it wasn't mistakes it was gambles—or maybe wrong decisions—by Brown.

Against the Packers, trailing by Green Bay's final winning margin of three points, the Bengals got to the seven-yard line, and the field goal team ran onto the field. But Paul Brown changed his mind, decided to go for a first down and saw his gamble fail. A practically "sure" field goal might have changed the complexion of the season.

A week later, trailing 17–3 against the Dolphins, the Bengals found themselves on the Miami one-yard line at fourth down. This time Paul did not gamble. He ordered a field goal, which was successful, bringing the score to 17–6. Miami won, 23–13, and second-guessers told Paul he should have tried for a touchdown. It was that kind of a season.

Vernon Holland braces himself to block Bob Briggs of Cleveland.

Cleveland dropped the Bengals 27–24 the following week, renewing the pattern in which enemy teams took quick advantage of Cincinnati mistakes, and then came another heartbreaking loss—31–27—to Oakland.

The Bengals got down to the absolute limit of quarterbacks in this one. Cook, of course, had not even started the season. Carter was out with a shoulder separation. And now Anderson, who had been going on sheer guts with a "hip-pointer," simply couldn't make it to the field in the fourth quarter with the game tied 24–24.

Dave Lewis, who had never before played in a regular-season game at quarterback, was rushed onto the field. The situation looked good, with the Bengals on the Oakland ten-yard line.

Two plays took them to the three-yard stripe. It was almost certain that, had either Carter or Anderson been playing, Paul Brown would have called a pass play. Instead, the order was for Lewis to run a rollout, a play made to order for a man his size. But it went for no gain.

The Bengals settled for a field goal, but the lead was short-lived. Oakland came right back with a touchdown drive and it was all over.

The next two games were horrors, two more losses—to make it seven in a row—to Houston (10–6) and Atlanta (9–6). The Houston game may have been the worst ever played by a Cincinnati team.

The Low Point

The Oilers won on a forty-eight-yard return of a pass interception, while the Bengals' offense literally collapsed. Later Paul Brown declared, "It was about as poor an exhibition as I've ever seen our team give. I am embarrassed."

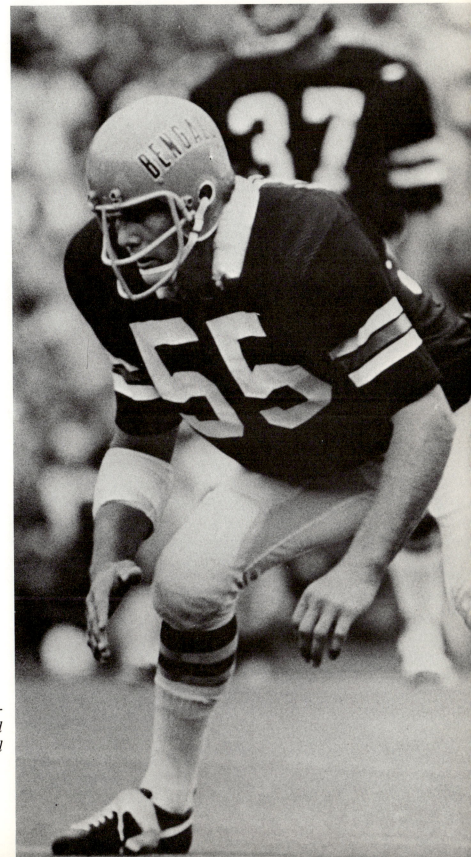

Paul Brown on Jim LeClair: "He's a rug-ged linebacker and has all the physical and mental attitudes to make it in professional football."

There were some shakeups before the Atlanta game, the biggest one being the release of Eric Crabtree who, in 1969, when Greg Cook had been around, had gained more than 700 yards on pass receptions. But nothing could substitute for the steady run of injuries that knocked out defensive tackle Steve Chomyszak, linebacker Bill Bergey, Mike Reid and even "old reliable," center Bob Johnson.

The Atlanta game, too, was another the Bengals should have won. But they didn't. Lady Luck is fickle. Late in the game, leading 6–3, Cincinnati stopped the Falcons at the two-yard line on four occasions. But the Falcs got the ball back with 1:54 left and won on a forty-six-yard pass from Dick Shiner to Art Malone. It didn't even matter that the extra point was blocked.

The turn-around finally came with a 24–10 victory over Denver, followed by a 28–13 gallop over Houston and, finally, a 31–0 romp over San Diego, a surprising victory second only to the demolition of Philadelphia that had opened the season. But the comeback was short-lived.

An early December date with the Browns at Cleveland ended in a familiarly frustrating defeat, 31–27. After that came successive losses to Pittsburgh and the Jets, and finally peace mercifully descended over the practice grounds at Spinney Field.

"I hope," Paul Brown said later, "that we never have to go through another season like that."

"our future... is bright"

Young quarterback Kenny Anderson is expected to battle Virgil Carter for leadership of the Bengals.

In the five-week period before the 1972 draft, Brown and his staff decided that the defense needed beefing up once more. In particular, they were interested in a big, strong and lightning-quick defensive end, and they knew where to look.

Their number-one pick was 270-pound Sherman White from the University of California, and, like all other Bengal first-round draft choices, he moved right into a starting assignment only three weeks after playing in the College All-Star game.

When the Bengals' second turn to draft came up, Brown couldn't believe his luck. Still available, probably only because scouts were sure he would select medical school over football, was Louisiana State's sensational All-America safety, Tommy Casanova.

One of the most explosive runners in foot-ball, lightning-quick Essex Johnson, led the Bengals in rushing in 1972.

Defensive end Sherman White, first-round draft pick from the University of California, led the young Bengal defense to an 8–6 record in his rookie year of 1972.

The Bengals hoped both players would be starters from the beginning, and White and Casanova concurred. As it turned out, all were right, and neither player missed a minute of field time in 1972.

But the Bengals' drive for defense, "which is where most games are decided, anyway," in Brown's opinion, went on. Linebacker Jim LeClair from North Dakota was chosen in the third round, and cornerback Bernard Jackson, who had been a standout halfback at Washington State in his junior and senior years, was fourth.

The Bengals were confident that they had pulled off another good draft year, as center-guard Tom DeLeone from Ohio State, wide receiver Dan Kratzer from Missouri Valley and tackle Stan Walters from Syracuse also made the roster.

Kratzer was taxied, but Walters became a regular late in the season after an injury to Rufus Mayes. And, finally, the Bengals had seventeenth-round draft choice Dave Green, a punter with remarkable potential, still around. Green's presence became more than just an accident at the end of the '72 season after Dave Lewis, the NFL's leading punter for two straight years, fell off a bit.

Paul Brown had made up his mind about one thing as the Bengals went back to Wilmington for their 1972 camp: There was to be no heavy emphasis on winning preseason games, as there had been the year before. He wanted the Bengals, in the last segment of his "five-year plan," to start the regular season as relaxed as possible— and, hopefully, free of injuries.

The exhibition season was just as formidable as ever, including the now traditional collision with the Browns that is of great interest to all Ohioans. The Bengals won that one, 27–21 and also beat Detroit and Philadelphia, losing to Green Bay, Miami and Atlanta.

As always, except for the first year's impossible match-up with San Diego, the Bengals were ready for their opener against New England in the Patriots' new stadium at Foxboro, Massachusetts. The starting quarterback assignment went to Ken Anderson, principally because he seemed possessed of a longer throwing arm. And, to repeat an old refrain, Greg Cook was still on the roster but still not around.

As the Bengals walked off with a 31–7 win in that opening game, the boos for the Patriots probably were heard in both Boston and Providence. The Bengals scored in every quarter and made a rout of the meeting.

But the next week, opening against Pittsburgh at Riverfront, the Bengals made a discovery: These weren't the same Steelers. They had a brutal defense, anchored by "Mean" Joe Greene, and their offense, under Terry Bradshaw and a hard core of rookies, was something else.

The Bengals won that one, 15–10, strictly on the strength of their field-goal ace Horst Muhlmann, who put five in a row between the uprights. But as Bill Bergey said later, "It's going to be something else when we have to meet them over there." He turned out to be a prophet.

Cleveland finally managed a "big win" over the Bengals in game number three. It was 27–6, easily the biggest margin of all their games, and the Bengals seemed never to be in it. Yet they remained unruffled.

With Anderson getting better with each game, and Carter either helping out when called on or coming in late like a short reliever in baseball, they made a tough combination.

Mike Reid stands in triumph after successfully tackling Denver quarterback Steve Ramsey.

Doug Dressler uses his six-foot-two, 228-pound frame to advantage as a good backfield blocker.

The Bengal defense gang tackles Cleveland's Leroy Kelly.

The Bengals swung by Denver and Kansas City, both by convincing, if not overwhelming, margins, and headed into Los Angeles to play the old, established Rams, a team they had never met before. Cincinnati stood at 4–1. It was the second-best record in pro football next to the Miami Dolphins, who were destined to go through an undefeated season.

"An Officiating Error"

As Paul Brown looked back at that 15–12 loss to Los Angeles, he was convinced that "that game started our downfall, and it was all due to an officiating error." Pictures later confirmed that the awarding of a safety to the Rams was completely in error.

Nevertheless, it wasn't entirely an officiating mistake. Horst Muhlmann, the hero of five field goals against the Steelers, missed three short-range attempts that could easily have won the game.

The Bengals recovered from that one with a 30–7 romp over Houston and now stood 5–2, but then they faced a return game with the ever-improving Steelers back in Pittsburgh. Remembering the first game, and what he had said afterward, Bill Bergey stated flatly, "We're in for something, but I think if we can win this game we can win the division championship."

The Bengals never came close. The Steelers routed them, 40–17, but Paul Brown later claimed that "our split with a fine Pittsburgh team was a real accomplishment as far as the season goes."

Then came a couple of heartbreakers, losses by 20–14 and 20–19 to Oakland and Baltimore, both before the home fans at Riverfront, and the Bengals evened the season at 5–5. They retained a slight chance to beat out the free-swinging Browns and Steelers, and kept alive on the next two Sundays with victories over long-time NFL teams, the Chicago Bears (13–3) and New York Giants (13–10). But the Browns and Steelers kept on winning, too.

After grabbing a touchdown pass, Chip Myers manages to hold on to the ball as the official signals the score.

In yet another of those dates with the Browns at Riverfront, it was the same old story. A late fumble gave Cleveland the ball, resulting in an even later touchdown and a typical victory for the Browns, 27–24. It was the *coup de grace* for the Bengals in the 1972 race, even though they had one game left to play.

With the pressure off, the Bengals headed for the finale against Houston, and it was strictly no contest. They put on their finest offensive show in history, and the defense added three touchdowns to the cause as they routed the Oilers, 61–17. It was a record score for both clubs, in victory for Cincinnati and in defeat for the hapless Houston horrors.

Surveying the Season

Paul Brown surveyed the season of 1972 and noted, "I thought we accomplished a lot. We beat two NFL 'landmark' teams in Chicago and New York and beat them worse than the scores show. I also think we started Kansas City on a downward tumble after we beat them. We're in the same division as Pittsburgh and Cleveland, and they'll continue to be strong. When Sid Gillman goes to Houston [as general manager], we expect him to make order out of chaos.

"The quarterbacks we've had in our developing years have been prime factors all the way through. Our future in pro football in Cincinnati is bright."

Running back Doug Dressler had his finest season in 1972, leading the Bengals in touchdowns scored by rushing. He also compiled enough yardage to become their number-two ground gainer.

Cincinnati linemen Steve Chomyszak (79) and Ron Carpenter (70) pursue Oiler quarterback Dan Pastorini.

the
bengals'
tigers

tommy casanova

With a vacancy at the deep safety spot, created by Sandy Durko's knee injury, there never was any doubt that rookie Tommy Casanova was ready to take his place with the greats of pro football when he came to the Bengals from LSU in 1972. He has more than lived up to the billing given him by *Sports Illustrated* beneath his cover photo a couple of years ago: "The Best College Football Player in the Land."

A tremendous athlete, a "bear for the football," his 9.7 sprinters' speed in the 100-yard dash and amazing reactions make Casanova as fine a prospect as ever came into the league. As a rookie in 1972, Tom equaled Parrish in interceptions with five, and ran 108 yards in returns. He pulled down thirty punts during the year, often fearlessly in the middle of a half dozen defenders, and got 289 yards on returns, one for his first touchdown as a pro. His lone kickoff return was good for thirty-four yards.

A handsome bachelor who is fond of horseback riding and "just plain fishin'," Casanova has been accepted at the University of Cincinnati Medical School and will be a student there in the offseason. His father is a doctor and the Casanova home town is Crowley, Louisiana.

In 1972, Casanova led the team in interceptions with five for 108 yards.

Tommy Casanova, sensational as a rookie, returns an interception against the Denver Broncos.

In 1972 Tommy Casanova was second in the AFC in punt returns with a 9.6 yard average.

*Tommy Casanova was an All-American at
Louisiana State and a second-round draft
pick of the Bengals in 1972.*

Free safety Tommy Casanova confers with Bengal defensive coach Chuck Studley.

In his first year with the Bengals, Tommy Casanova performed with excellence at safety, a position usually very difficult for a rookie to handle.

Few professional athletes pursue a second career in the field of music. Mike Reid is, surprisingly, a concert pianist as well as an outstanding defensive tackle.

mike reid

Mike Reid must rank as the most dynamic person, both on and off the field, on the Bengals' roster. Already a two-time All-Pro in just three years, the brilliantly effective defensive tackle ranks as high in the brain league as does teammate Virg Carter. Reid's forte is the piano and musical composition. He has played in many symphony orchestras, makes frequent appearances with the highly regarded Cincinnati Symphony and has composed pieces that range from classical to country.

But what this guy doesn't do in music, he does on the football field. A classical-music "square" is not often a popular man on a football team, but Reid is. His play, his drive and his strength say it all. "The guy is a constant inspiration to me," says Royce Berry, the Bengals' "Mr. Consistency," who plays next to Reid at left end. "And he makes things easier for us, too. If they two-time Mike, something has to give somewhere else."

Reid's task was made just a little easier in 1972—if a defensive lineman's job is ever easy—by the acquisition of defensive end Sherman White. Big Sherm often needs two-timing himself, and, when he gets it, Reid simply devastates anyone playing him one-on-one.

Mike Reid defiantly waits for the opposition . . .

. . . and then pulls down a Denver runner just short of the goal line.

Lemar Parrish heads upfield with an interception against the Cleveland Browns.

Star cornerback Lemar Parrish intercepted five passes in 1972. He carried two of them for touchdowns.

lemar parrish

A two-time selectee for the Pro Bowl in 1970 and 1971, Bengal cornerback Lemar Parrish has blazing speed and quickness that continually amaze his personal coach, Chuck Weber. Playing a position that calls for excessive skills and is watched by every fan every week, Parrish—like all players who ply his trade—is fair game for the "boo birds" when he makes a mistake. He is seldom booed.

Parrish had one big problem in 1972: he coughed up the ball on key situations on punt or kickoff returns. Yet he returned fifteen kickoffs for 348 yards and fifteen punts for 141, once breaking it all the way for the eighth touchdown of his pro career. Aggressive and alert on pass defense, he came up with five interceptions for ninety yards and two touchdowns. A product of tiny Lincoln University, he pairs with Ken Riley at cornerback. Between "Leapin' Lemar," as he calls himself, and "The Rattler," as the Bengals call Riley, there aren't many better cornerbacks around.

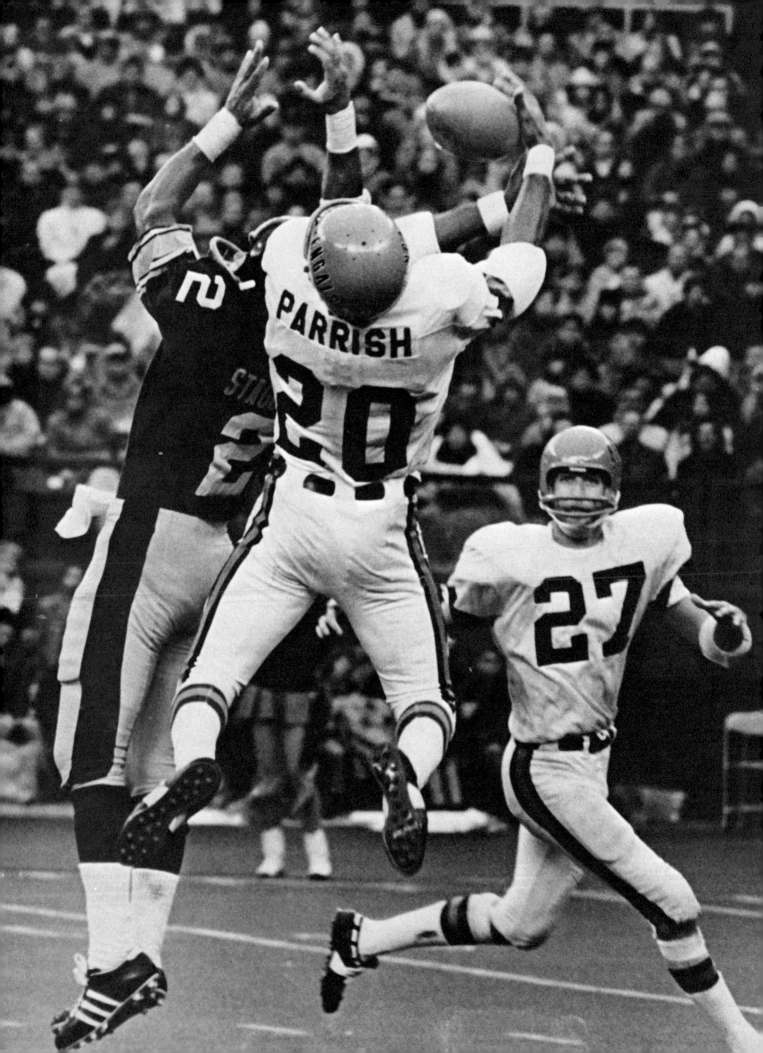

Paul Brown on Lemar Parrish: "He accelerates faster than any player I've ever coached."

Lemar Parrish, a Pro Bowl player in 1971 and 1972, breaks up a pass intended for Jon Staggers, then a Steeler.

Placekicker Horst Muhlmann from West Germany is the Bengals' top scorer and one of the better field goal kickers in the NFL.

Placekicker Horst Muhlmann succeeded on twenty-seven of forty field goal attempts in 1972.

horst muhlmann

No analysis of the Bengals' potential can be allowed to pass without reference to the kicking game, and soccer-style placekicker Horst Muhlmann has made an extra valuable contribution during his four-year tenure.

"Der Horst," as Cincinnati's German population likes to call Muhlmann, is an emotional guy with great pride, and he is not happy with the 1972 season, in which he missed thirteen of forty field goals and one of thirty-one extra points. But he is philosophical and tries not to let it get him down.

Horst most certainly has won more games than he has lost for Cincinnati, and opposing teams have genuine respect for his range and accuracy. Although he has not yet mastered English completely, Muhlmann gets along extremely well with his teammates. During the offseason Horst, his wife and two children visit family and friends in West Germany. He returns for training camp in July, bringing his family back to the United States when school begins in September.

115

ken anderson

Ken Anderson, the quiet, unimposing and now maturing young man from Augustana, thrown into the breach far sooner than he should have been, went into the 1973 season as starting quarterback. "As far as I'm concerned," Paul Brown says of him, "Kenny is way beyond three far more widely heralded and highly sought quarterbacks in the league, Dan Pastorini, Jim Plunkett and Archie Manning. He is physically their equal or better, and he has a fine mind."

Anderson received his degree in mathematics at Augustana in 1972, having continued his schooling after turning pro. He is a serious, soft-spoken young man, cut from much the same mold as Virg Carter, and is rapidly attaining a reputation as a good guy. For months he seemed to stand in awe of Carter; now all that is passing. And his football-passing ability speaks for itself.

He had the lowest percentage of interceptions in the AFC in the 1972 season and ranked fifth in the overall rating of conference quarterbacks. He has completed 55 percent of his passes for two successive seasons and is a study in consistency.

At the start of the 1973 season, Ken Anderson was considered Cincinnati's number-one quarterback.

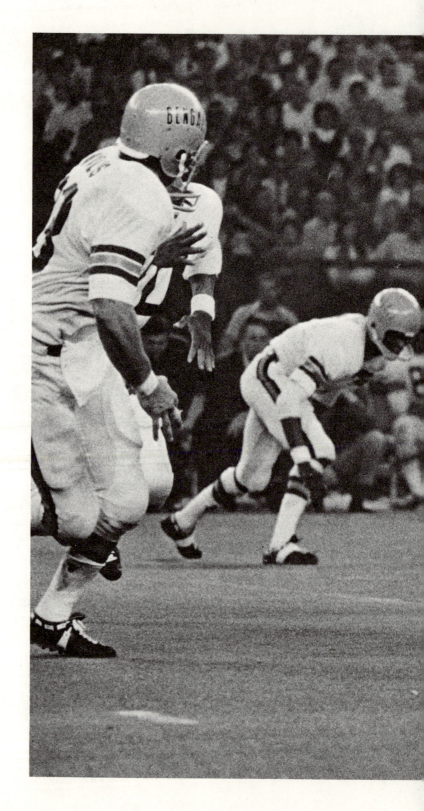

Paul Brown says of his young, unheralded quarterback, Ken Anderson: "Kenny is way beyond far more highly sought quarterbacks Dan Pastorini, Jim Plunkett or Archie Manning."

Wide receiver Charlie Joiner goes into motion while quarterback Ken Anderson prepares to take the snap.

Some thought that inexperienced Ken Anderson was not ready to become a starting quarterback so early in his career. He proved the cynics wrong.

bob trumpy
chip myers

Wide receiver Bob Trumpy, here applying ice to injured fingers, has become one of the most feared pass catchers in the game.

Chip Myers repeated this triumphal gesture two other times in 1972 after brilliant touchdown catches.

At six-foot-six and six-foot-five, respectively, tight end Bob Trumpy and wide receiver Chip Myers give the Bengals two of the tallest passing targets in football. They are both blond, often mistaken for each other, and have similar moves and speed, although Trumpy is called on for some extraordinary blocking duty at times.

After breaking both arms, which kept him out of a few early-season games in 1971, Myers, a product of Northwest Oklahoma State who was originally drafted by the San Francisco 49ers in 1967, really came into his own in 1972.

Chip caught a club-record fifty-seven passes for 792 yards and three touchdowns, second only—by one catch—to Oakland's Fred Biletnikoff in the entire league. A casual guy with a slow grin, Chip was honored by being selected for the AFC squad in the Pro Bowl, the first time he's made the post-season game.

Trumpy, whose alma mater is Utah, was All-Pro and made the old AFL All-Star team his first year, 1968, returning in 1969. The big, rangy guy with long arms and legs hauled in forty-four passes in 1972, surpassing his previous year's record of forty. His receptions were good for exactly 500 yards, including two touchdowns.

Despite his selection as All-AFC tight end in 1970, he was switched to an outside position in mid-season of 1971 to put more diversification in the attack—it paid off handsomely. This allowed Bruce Coslet to move in at tight end and gave the Bengals a receiving corps of six-foot-six, six-foot-five and six-foot-three, the tallest in football.

Sometimes outspoken, always ready with a comment or a wisecrack, Bob Trumpy has become one of the most feared tight ends–wide receivers in the NFL. "Trump" hopes to take the Bengals all the way in 1973.

In his quest for yardage, Chip Myers hurdles Cleveland's Ben Davis.

Chip Myers gathers in a pass and attempts to elude the fast-closing Ben Davis of Cleveland.

Although not illustrated here, wide receiver Chip Myers was fourth in receiving in the NFL in 1972.

Chip Myers (25) was the AFC's third leading pass receiver in 1972. Here he fakes a move to Oakland's All-Pro defensive back Willie Brown.

In 1971, Bob Trumpy led the Bengals in pass receiving.

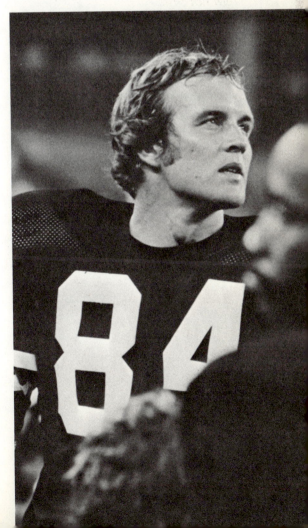

Bob Trumpy holds on to the ball as he is brought down by Miami's Mike Kolen.

Myers is difficult to down after he catches a ball, as exemplified by this struggle with a Houston defensive back.

Wide receiver Bob Trumpy heads toward the end zone after tripping up Giant defenders.

The Bengals' drive to the 1970 AFC Central Division championship came after Virgil Carter took over the quarterback job.

virg carter

As it is with most football teams, the quarterback position at Cincinnati is always a focal point. And the men who have played there have been and are outstanding players.

Gutsy, quiet, confident Virg Carter probably never has received the credit due him, but it is no accident that the Bengals' drive to the AFC Central Division championship in 1970 came after Carter took over as quarterback.

Courage is Carter's trademark. He has often played more seriously hurt than any quarterback ought to be. It is not as easy for a quarterback to "play hurt" as it is for a tackle or linebacker. The job demands perfection. Carter's one limitation has been difficulty in throwing the long ball with consistency. But there is no better passer from the standpoint of accuracy if you tailor the offense to his skills.

In 1970, still just learning Paul Brown's system, Carter improved his passing accuracy to better than 51 percent and additionally ran for 246 yards and scored two touchdowns. The next season, he completed a fantastic 138 of 222 passes for 62 percent, including ten touchdowns, and his percentage of completions in 1972, when he played behind Anderson, was still a remarkable 57 percent.

Carter has a tremendous mind. An engineering science major at Brigham Young, he earned both a master's and a doctorate at Northwestern and, during the offseason, taught mathematics at Xavier University. He has authored a serious football book on "play probability."

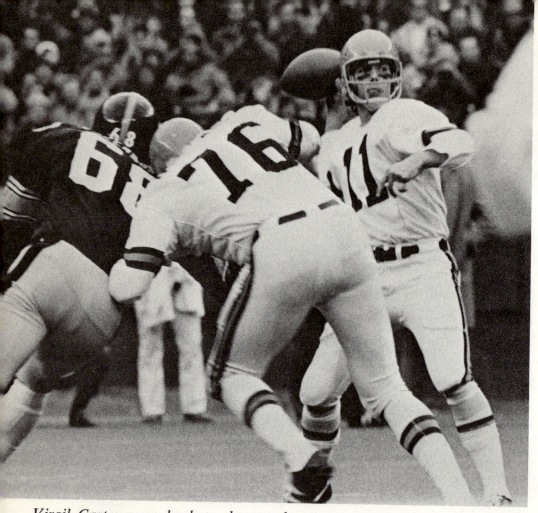

Virgil Carter rears back to throw a long pass. If he has one flaw, it's inconsistency in throwing the big pass.

Quarterback Virgil Carter was the most accurate passer in the NFL in 1971, completing 62.2 of his passes. Ten resulted in touchdowns.

bob
johnson

Often overlooked by everyone is Bob Johnson, a man who has centered the ball for the quarterback in every play in regular-season competition since the Bengals started. Quiet and unassuming but possessed of all the requisites, Johnson has the finesse of a ballet dancer but the power of a runaway freight car. Bob played the last half of the 1972 season with a bad back, the pain going down his leg and into his foot, and he was frequently subbed for by rookie Tom DeLeone in placekick or punting situations.

Johnson is a model citizen, advancing rapidly upward as a businessman in Cincinnati in the offseason. He belongs to the Fellowship of Christian Athletes, as do many of the Bengals, and gives literally hundreds of speeches each year to church, civic and youth groups.

Center Bob Johnson leads blocking on a kick return for a slanting Bernard Jackson.

Center Bob Johnson was an original Bengal, the first college player to be drafted by the team.

essex johnson

If Bob Johnson is the hub of the offensive line, Essex Johnson has come into his own as a running back. The "Essex Express" or "Mr. Big Play," as he is called, really blossomed in 1971, when Paul Brown used him at strategic times when the enemy appeared just a bit tired. It paid off. He broke through the middle on swirling, twirling touchdown runs of eighty-six, sixty-eight, sixty-seven and forty-one yards, and gained 522 yards on eighty-five carries for a sizzling 6.1 yards-per-carry average.

Only five-feet-nine and 197 pounds, Ess is easily the fastest man on the team, with the possible exception of Tom Casanova or Lemar Parrish. He has remarkable balance and coordination.

A product of Grambling, Johnson was a sixth-round draft choice in 1968 and is one of the few remaining "original Bengals," as is Bob Johnson. Ess won a starting assignment for himself, carried more often and saw his average go down accordingly. But his value to the team is not just in running the ball. An excellent receiver, he often breaks out of the backfield to make key catches on which, frequently, he shakes loose for long runs or even touchdowns. His acceleration is as good as that of any back in the NFL. Essex Johnson has made a mighty contribution to the Bengals' success.

It doesn't seem as if anyone will be impeding the progress of Bengal runner Essex Johnson, as well protected as he is by three linemen.

The Bengal defense gang tackles a New Orleans runner.

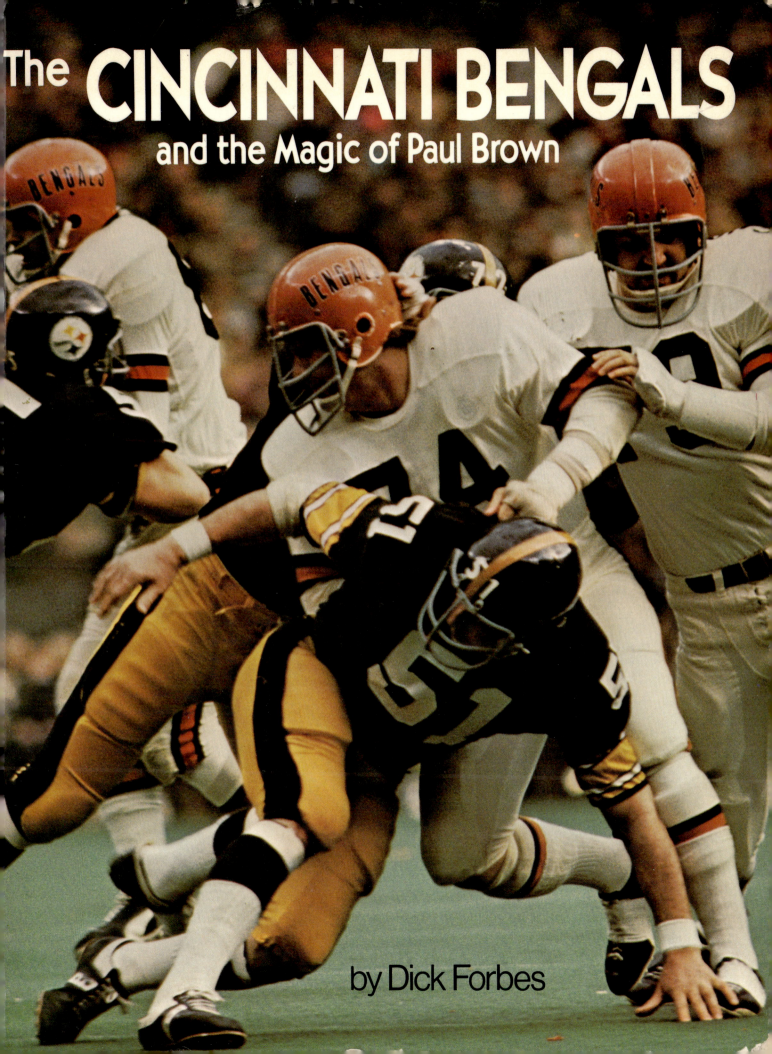

The CINCINNATI BENGALS
and the Magic of Paul Brown

by Dick Forbes